DINOSAURS

A Coloring and Activity Book for Kids

This book belongs to:

_____

My favorite dinosaur is:

_____

Copyright © 2019 Caitlin Monachino
All Rights Reserved
ISBN-13: 978-1950601011
ISBN-10: 1950601013

Name: Allosaurus
Pronounced: ALE-oh-SORE-us
Meaning: "other lizard"
Diet: Carnivore
Size: Giant
Length: 25 to 35 feet
Height: 17 to 20 feet

Name: Archaeopteryx
Pronounced: ARK-ee-OP-turr-icks
Meaning: "ancient wing"
Diet: Carnivore
Size: Small
Length: Up to 20 inches
Height: 20 to 24 inches

Name: Ankylosaurus
Pronounced: AN-kee-lo-SORE-us
Meaning: "stiff lizard"
Diet: Herbivore
Size: Giant
Length: 35 feet
Height: 4 feet at hips

Name: Dilophosaurus
Pronounced: die-LOW-fuh-SORE-us
Meaning: "two-ridged lizard"
Diet: Carnivore
Size: Large
Length: 20 feet
Height: Up to 7 feet

Name: Compsognathus
Pronounced: KOMP-sog-NAH-thus
Meaning: "pretty jaw"
Diet: Carnivore
Size: Small
Length: 2 feet
Height: 10 inches at the hips

Name: Diplodocus
Pronounced: dih-PLOD-uh-kus
Meaning: "double beam"
Diet: Herbivore
Size: Wow!
Length: 90 to 175 feet
Height: Up to 22 feet

Name: Mosasaurus
Pronounced: MOE-zah-SORE-us
Meaning: "Meuse lizard"
Diet: Carnivore
Size: Giant
Length: 50 feet
Height: 10 feet

Name: Velociraptor
Pronounced: vel-OSS-uh-rap-ter
Meaning: "speedy thief"
Diet: Carnivore
Size: Small
Length: Up to 7 feet
Height: Up to 2 feet at the hips

Name: Triceratops
Pronounced: tri-SAIR-uh-tops
Meaning: "three-horned face"
Diet: Herbivore
Size: Giant
Length: 30 feet
Height: 10 feet

Name: Tyrannosaurus rex
Pronounced: tye-RAN-uh-SORE-us rex
Meaning: "king of the tyrant lizards"
Diet: Carnivore
Size: Giant
Length: 40 feet
Height: 15 to 20 feet

Name: Stegosaurus
Pronounced: STEG-uh-SORE-us
Meaning: "roofed lizard"
Diet: Herbivore
Size: Large
Length: 23 to 30 feet
Height: 9 feet

Name: Spinosaurus
Pronounced: SPINE-oh-SORE-us
Meaning: "spine lizard"
Diet: Carnivore
Size: Giant
Length: 41 to 59 feet
Height: Unknown

Name: Pteranodon
Pronounced: ter-AN-uh-don
Meaning: "toothless wing"
Diet: Pescivore / Carnivore
Size: Medium
Length: 18 feet
Height: 6 feet

Name: Parasaurolophus
Pronounced: pair-uh-suh-ROL-uff-us
Meaning: "crested lizard"
Diet: Herbivore
Size: Giant
Length: 40 feet
Height: 8 feet tall at the hips

Name: Plesiosaurus
Pronounced: PLEE-see-oh-SORE-us
Meaning: "almost lizard"
Diet: Piscivore / Carnivore
Size: Medium
Length: 12 to 15 feet
Height: 4 feet

Name: Pachycephalosaurus
Pronounced: pack-ee-SEF-ah-lo-SORE-us
Meaning: "thick-headed lizard"
Diet: Herbivore
Size: Medium
Length: 15 feet
Height: 17.5 feet

Name: Iguanodon
Pronounced: ig-WAN-uh-don
Meaning: "iguana toothed"
Diet: Herbivore
Size: Giant
Length: 45 feet
Height: 16 feet

Name: Majungasaurus
Pronounced: muh-JUN-guh-SORE-us
Meaning: "Majungha lizard"
Diet: Carnivore
Size: Large
Length: 20 to 23 feet
Height: Unknown

Name: Corythosaurus
Pronounced: co-RITH-oh-SORE-us
Meaning: "helmet lizard"
Diet: Herbivore
Size: Giant
Length: 33 feet
Height: 7 feet at the hips

Name: Acanthopholis
Pronounced: ah-can-THOFF-oh-liss
Meaning: "spiny scales"
Diet: Herbivore
Size: Medium
Length: 10 to 18 feet
Height: Unknown

Connect the dots by tracing from one number to the next and then circle the name of the dinosaur you uncover!

Brontosaurus **Triceratops**

Ankylosaurus

Match the dinosaurs to their shadows!

Each row of dinosaur eggs follows a different pattern. Fill in the missing numbers and letters!

2 — 4 — 6 — ⬚ — 10 — 12

1 — 3 — ⬚ — 7 — 9 — 11

A — C — E — G — ⬚ — K

Z — ⬚ — V — T — R — P

Help the Pterodactyl find its way through the clouds!

Use the color key to color in the amber fossil.

1 = Purple
2 = Blue
3 = Yellow
4 = Orange
5 = Red-Orange
6 = Red

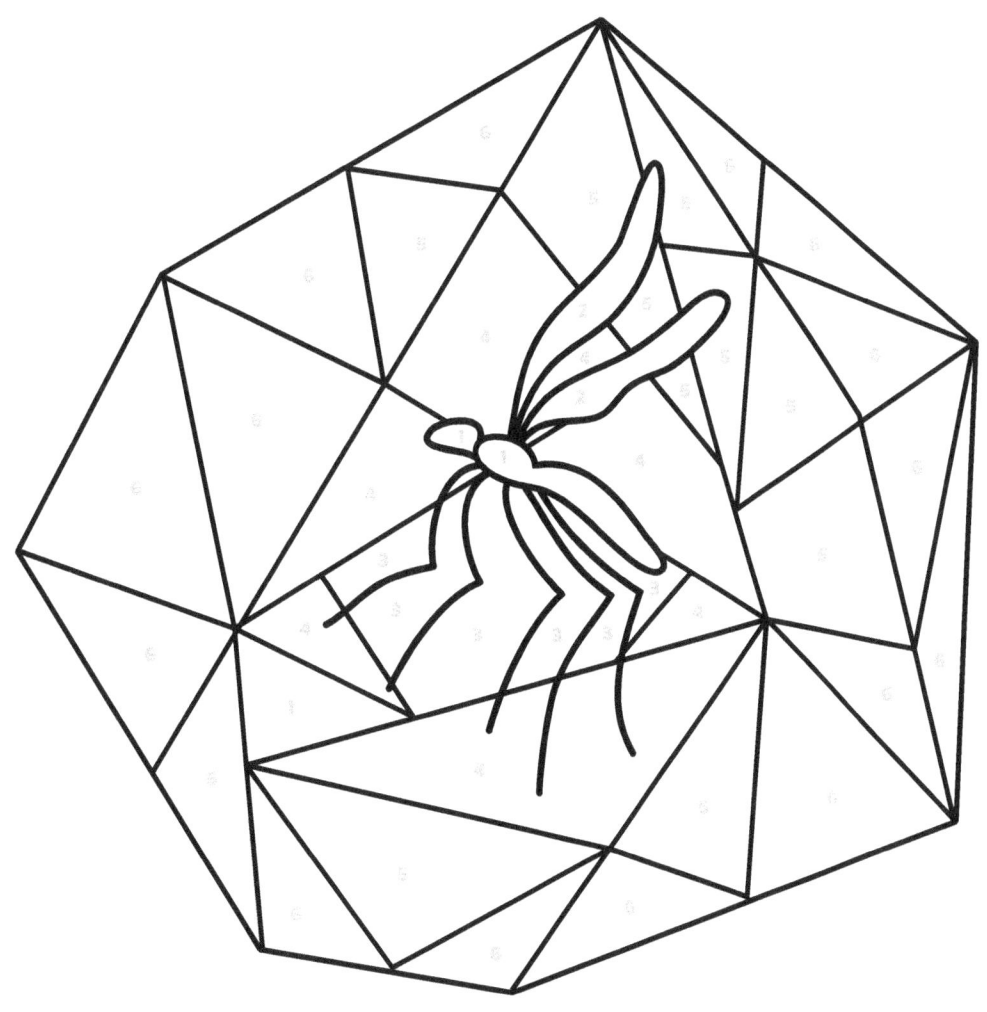

How many words can you make with the letters in "dinosaurs"?

DINOSAURS

SOAR

RAINS

Circle 4 differences between the two triceratops below!

Herbivores are animals that eat plants. Draw your favorite foods!

Play Tic-Tac-Toe with a friend!

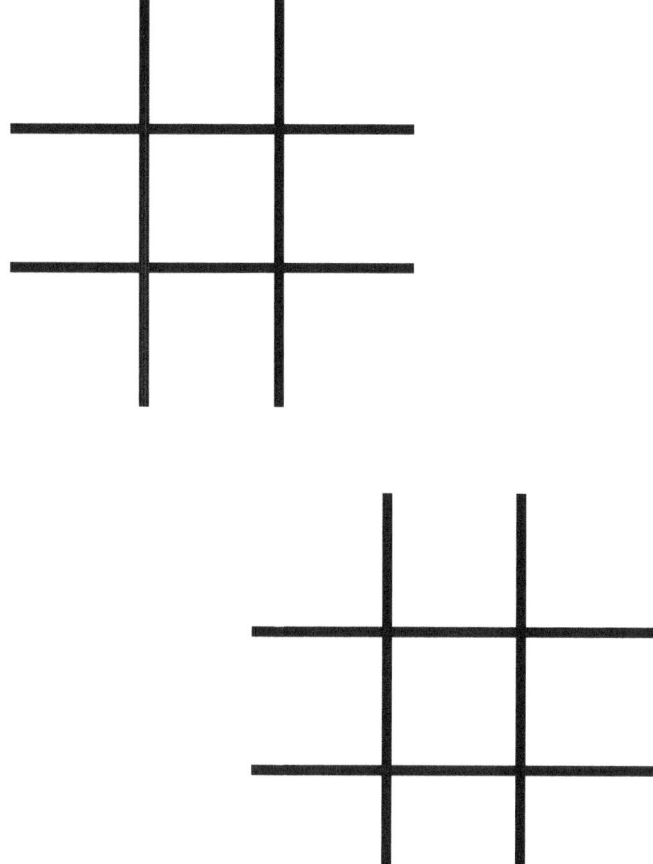

Can you find these words in the grid below? The words may be spelled vertically, horizontally, backwards or diagonally.

- EXTINCT
- VOLCANO
- FOSSIL
- JURASSIC
- BONES
- MASSIVE
- CLAWS
- PREHISTORIC

```
N O N A C L O V G C E C
M A S S I V E U S D B I
C Z G S Y M I U I M O S
H L S A J E Z O B Y N S
F O A N T C N I T X E A
F Y Q W N A J I R S R
S D T V S O Y L F H A U
P R E H I S T O R I C J
W O N N T W B S P W W N
```

Count the number of dinosaur eggs. Write the number in the box.

Help the Stegosaurus mommy reunite with her baby!

Fill in the blanks below by unscrambling the letters to finish the short story.

The ___ (NSU) was shining bright over the arid desert landscape. There was no ____ (ARNI) for weeks and the dinosaurs who lived there were very thirsty. One brave little dinosaur traveled long and far through the ____ (DANS) in search of water. Finally, he came upon a _____ (NUORD) pool surrounded by lush plants and creatures of all kinds. He ___ (ARN) back to tell his dinosaur friends that he found a watering hole. It was a dinosaur dash! They would zip and zoom, whirl and whoosh, some would scurry and some would ____ (ROSA), all in a race to the _____ (AIOSS).

Turn the page for a bonus question!

Bonus Question: What do all of the scrambled words have in common?

Finish the sentence using the code below!

E =    A =

R =    S =

M =    T =

Some dinosaurs, like the Tyrannosaurus rex, are carnivores. Carnivores are also known as...

__ __ __ __

__ __ __ __ __ __

Help the dinosaur escape the volcano!

FINISH

A

B

C

36

Design your own dinosaur egg!

Color the velociraptors then circle the one that does not match!

Can you find these words in the grid below? The words may be spelled vertically, horizontally, backwards or diagonally.

- LAVA
- TRIASSIC
- ROAR
- TEETH
- DINOSAUR
- SKELETON
- PREDATOR
- FOOTPRINTS

```
D A Z W Q S A Z R B Z F
P I O N N A K V C O V I
R E N E O U V M A Q A R
E D K O H T E E T L X R
D V Y J S V E H D D V U
A T T H Z A E L V K N A
T H T E H F U I E H P U
O C I S S A I R T K B Q
R F O O T P R I N T S E
```

SOLUTIONS!

Page 23

Page 24

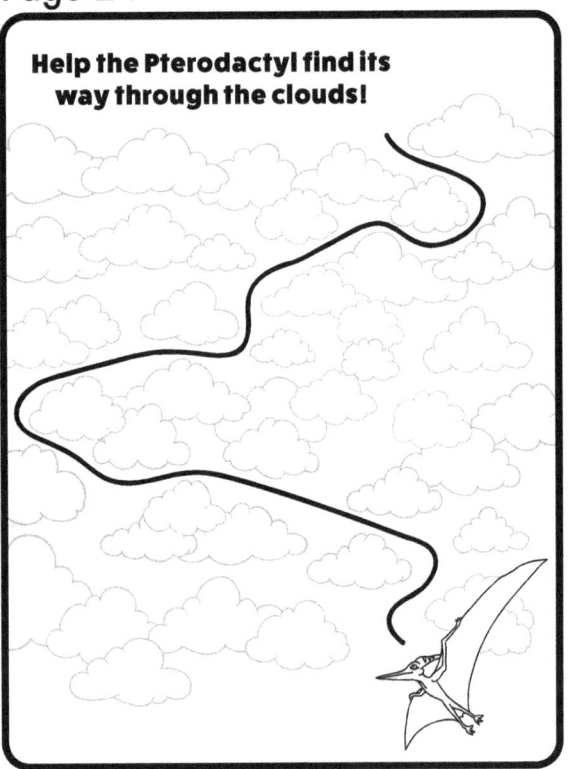

Page 27

Page 30

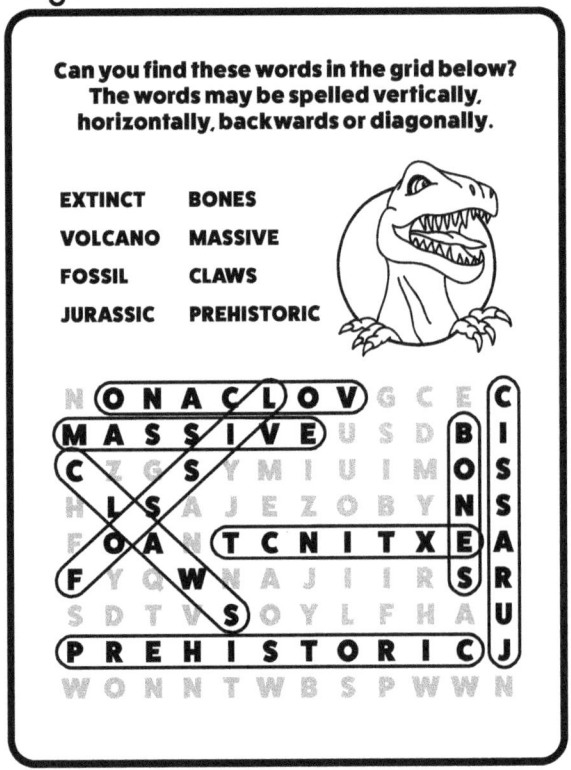

Page 31

Count the number of dinosaur eggs. Write the number in the box.

Page 32

Help the Stegosaurus mommy reunite with her baby!

Page 33

Fill in the blanks below by unscrambling the letters to finish the short story.

The **SUN** was shining bright over the arid desert landscape. There was no **RAIN** for weeks and the dinosaurs who lived there were very thirsty. One brave little dinosaur traveled long and far through the **SAND** in search of water. Finally, he came upon a **ROUND** pool surrounded by lush plants and creatures of all kinds. He **RAN** back to tell his dinosaur friends that he found a watering hole. It was a dinosaur dash! They would zip and zoom, whirl and whoosh, some would scurry and some would **SOAR**, all in a race to the **OASIS**.

Bonus answer: All of the words can be made out of the letters in DINOSAURS!

Page 34

A paleontologist is a scientist that studies fossils. These are some of the tools they use. Can you find them in the picture below?

Page 35

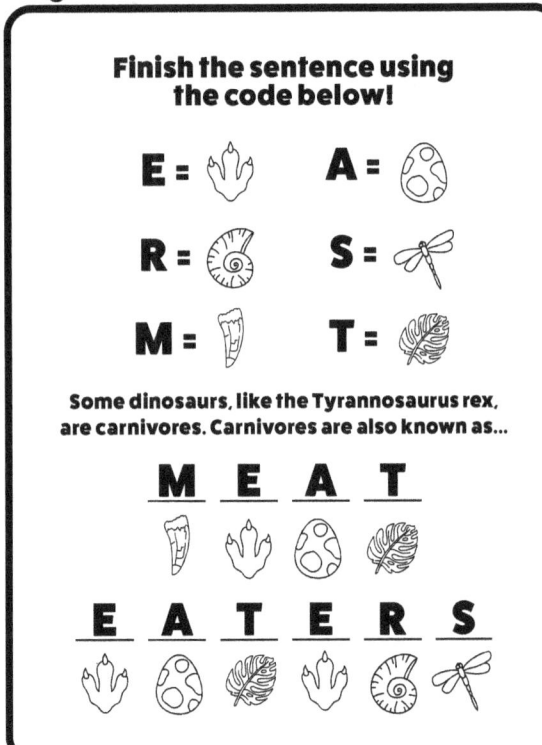

Page 36

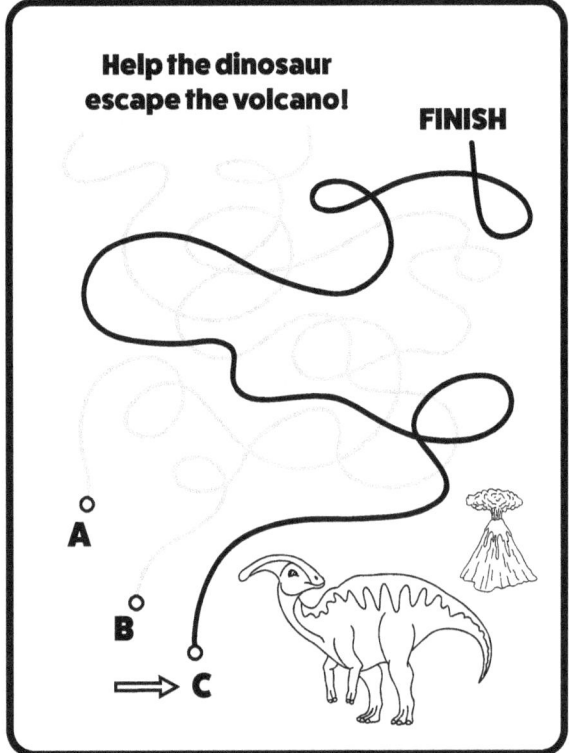

Page 38

Page 39

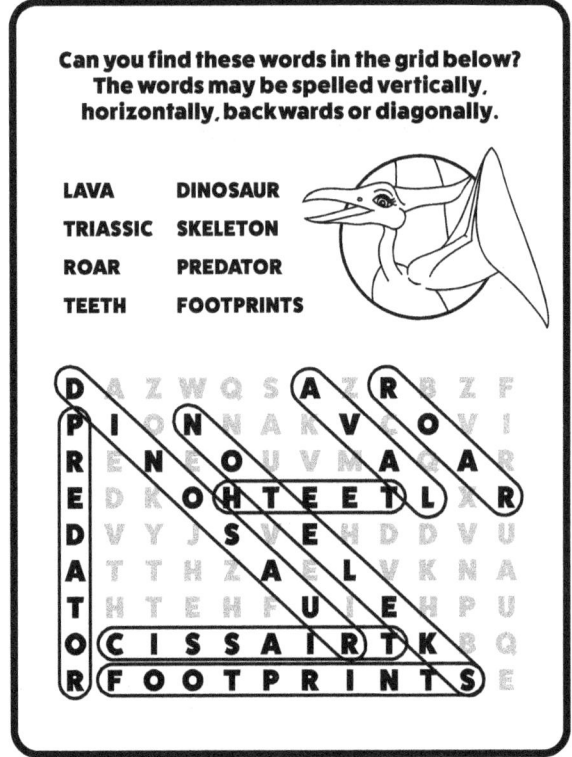

What do you call worried dinosaurs?

Nervous rex!

I hope you enjoyed the book!

www.ingramcontent.com/pod-product-compliance
Lightning Source LLC
Chambersburg PA
CBHW081018040426
42444CB00014B/3259